Samuel French Acting Edition

The Committee Meeting

A Comedy for Five Women in One Act

by Joellen K. Bland

SAMUELFRENCH.COM   SAMUELFRENCH.CO.UK

Copyright © 1968 by Walter H. Baker Company
All Rights Reserved

THE COMMITTEE MEETING is fully protected under the copyright laws of the United States of America, the British Commonwealth, including Canada, and all other countries of the Copyright Union. All rights, including professional and amateur stage productions, recitation, lecturing, public reading, motion picture, radio broadcasting, television and the rights of translation into foreign languages are strictly reserved.

ISBN 978-0-874-40914-7

www.SamuelFrench.com
www.SamuelFrench.co.uk

FOR PRODUCTION ENQUIRIES

UNITED STATES AND CANADA
Info@SamuelFrench.com
1-866-598-8449

UNITED KINGDOM AND EUROPE
Plays@SamuelFrench.co.uk
020-7255-4302

Each title is subject to availability from Samuel French, depending upon country of performance. Please be aware that *THE COMMITTEE MEETING* may not be licensed by Samuel French in your territory. Professional and amateur producers should contact the nearest Samuel French office or licensing partner to verify availability.

CAUTION: Professional and amateur producers are hereby warned that *THE COMMITTEE MEETING* is subject to a licensing fee. Publication of this play(s) does not imply availability for performance. Both amateurs and professionals considering a production are strongly advised to apply to Samuel French before starting rehearsals, advertising, or booking a theatre. A licensing fee must be paid whether the title(s) is presented for charity or gain and whether or not admission is charged. Professional/Stock licensing fees are quoted upon application to Samuel French.

No one shall make any changes in this title(s) for the purpose of production. No part of this book may be reproduced, stored in a retrieval system, or transmitted in any form, by any means, now known or yet to be invented, including mechanical, electronic, photocopying, recording, videotaping, or otherwise, without the prior written permission of the publisher. No one shall upload this title(s), or part of this title(s), to any social media websites.

For all enquiries regarding motion picture, television, and other media rights, please contact Samuel French.

Please refer to page 19 for further copyright information.

STORY OF THE PLAY

Sue and her committee get together to plan the church congregational dinner-meeting. While she tries to guide the discussion (often with the aid of a toy whistle to restore order) Amy prattles, Edith complains, Doris preaches and Mary amiably agrees with just about everything. They willingly offer comments, ideas and suggestions. However, when they are asked to assume responsibility, each responds with a prompt excuse for not accepting, and volunteers the time and services of someone else.

Most active women have been to committee meetings very much like this one.

CHARACTERS

AMY, *who offers everyone else's time and talents.*
EDITH, *who complains about everyone and everything.*
DORIS, *who talks a lot and does very little.*
MARY, *who agrees with just about everything.*
SUE, *who is chairman of the committee.*

SCENE: SUE'S *living room, where a committee meeting is being held.*
TIME: *Now.*

The Committee Meeting

SCENE: SUE'S *living room. As the play begins* AMY *and* MARY *sit together on one side of the room.* EDITH *and* DORIS *sit together on the opposite side.* SUE, *as chairman, sits in the center of the room. They may sit around a table or in living room chairs. Everyone except* SUE *is chattering noisily. After a moment* SUE *looks up from her list of notes and tries to get everyone's attention, but she is ignored.*

SUE.

Girls! Girls! It's time we began our meeting. Girls! (*As everyone continues chattering, she takes up a child's toy whistle, either from the table or from a cord around her neck, and blows a sharp blast. Everyone jumps and faces her with startled expressions.*) Girls, we have a lot of things to discuss tonight about the plans for the congregational dinner-meeting. But first, let's open our meeting with a word of prayer. (*All bow heads.*) Our dear Heavenly Father, we thank You for the opportunity to meet together and give of ourselves for Your work in our church. Be with us now as we plan for this meeting, and may we all stand ready to serve You willingly in whatever ways we can. Amen.

AMY.

(*To* MARY.) Oh, wasn't that a *lovely* prayer? Sue always gives such *lovely* prayers. I always say if you want someone to offer a *lovely* prayer, just call on Sue.

MARY.

Yes, yes! I quite agree.

SUE.

Now, before we go any further, I'd like someone to please take notes for me.

THE COMMITTEE MEETING

(*Everyone glances slyly at everyone else.*)

AMY.

(*Suddenly.*) Oh, Edith, why don't you? You always take such *nice* notes!

MARY.

Yes, yes! Edith should be the one to take the notes.

DORIS.

By all means! I take terrible notes. I can't remember a thing anyone says.

AMY.

Neither can I. I've never been secretary of anything.

MARY.

I was secretary of the Drama Club once, and oh, it was such a job!

EDITH.

(*Grouchily.*) Well, I don't have a pencil or any paper . . .

SUE.

Oh, I'll be glad to loan you a pencil, Edith. (*Hands her a pencil.*)

DORIS.

And I have some paper right here in my purse. (*Hands paper to* EDITH.)

AMY.

You always take such nice *neat* notes, Edith. I always say if you want someone to take nice *neat* notes, just call on Edith.

MARY.

Oh, yes! I quite agree!

EDITH.

Well, as long as no one else will . . .

SUE.

Thank you, Edith. Now, the work for this dinner-meeting has been divided into committees, and . . .

AMY.

Oh, committees are so *efficient*, don't you think? I always say there's nothing quite as *efficient* as a committee.

MARY.

Yes, yes! You're so right, Amy.

SUE.

I think it's a fine idea to combine a pitch-in dinner with the meeting this time. But it's going to take some work.

DORIS.

Well, I'm sure we're all ready to do our part. Why else would we five have been asked to do the planning for something as vital to the life of our church as a congregational meeting?

SUE.

Yes, there's so much that we women can do to make the meeting a success.

EDITH.

It's about time they turned things over to us women. *We* know how to get things done!

DORIS.

Whenever duty calls, we women must stand ready to answer. If this congregational meeting is to be long remembered as a landmark in the upward march of achievement in our church, we women must be responsible! (*Stands.*) *We* must take the lead! *We* must set the example! *We* must hear the call and obey! Nothing must sway us from this noble goal!

MARY.

Hear! Hear!

(*Everyone nods in agreement and claps vigorously.*)

AMY.

Oh, Doris, you make such *elegant* speeches. Just *elegant!* I always say if you need someone to make an *elegant* speech, just call on Doris.

MARY.

Yes, yes! I agree one hundred percent, Amy! One hundred percent!

DORIS.

Madame Chairman, we are all waiting to be called to service! (*Salutes and sits down.*)

SUE.

That's fine, girls. Now, the first item on my list is the Food Committee. We need some women to do calling and arrange for even distribution of the food.

EDITH.

Well, it's about time somebody thought of that. We always end up with such a lop-sided array of food, and we never have enough tables.

MARY.

At the last pitch-in we had too much macaroni and cheese and hardly any devilled eggs.

SUE.

Some people insist on bringing the same thing every time. We need more variety.

EDITH.

Well, I always bring macaroni and cheese because that's my specialty.

DORIS.

So do I. Everyone adores *my* macaroni and cheese.

MARY.

But there weren't enough devilled eggs last time, and I dearly love devilled eggs!

SUE.

I usually bring a cake because I have some absolutely delicious recipes for unusual cakes.

DORIS.

Well, I *always* bring macaroni and cheese!

EDITH.

(*Glaring at* DORIS.) Well, you needn't bother this time, because *I'm* going to bring the macaroni and cheese!

SUE.

I think I'll try that chocolate peppermint pistachio nut cake.

MARY.

Isn't anyone going to bring devilled eggs?

(*Everyone begins chattering and arguing noisily until* SUE *remembers that she is the chairman.*)

SUE.

Girls! Girls! (*As everyone ignores her, she blows on the whistle and everyone jumps and faces her.*) Girls, I'm sure we're all aware that a Food Committee is definitely needed. We'll elect a chairman in just a few minutes. The next item on my list is Decorations.

EDITH.

Well, I hope somebody can think of something original this time. I get so sick and tired of crêpe paper streamers flying all over the place. Why can't somebody around here use a little imagination?

DORIS.

Well, I might remind you, Edith, that we do have a limited budget for that kind of thing, and crêpe paper is inexpensive, fireproof, easy to work with, and comes in assorted colors. And there are lots of imaginative and creative uses for crêpe paper. You can crinkle it, twist it, cut it, feather it, fringe it, loop it, and stretch it— among other things!

AMY.

Fresh-cut flowers are always nice for springtime.

MARY.

Oh, yes! In bud vases or rose bowls or . . .

AMY.

And parasols! I *love* little parasols, especially in the springtime.

MARY.

Yes, yes! Little parasols!

EDITH.

There'll be men at this meeting, remember. Men don't like parasols!

AMY.

Oh, but parasols are so *quaint!* I always say there's nothing *quainter* than a little parasol!

DORIS.

And nothing as versatile, practical and economical as colored crêpe paper!

SUE.

Keep the ideas coming, girls. I'm sure we can come up with something pleasing to everyone.

EDITH.

(*To herself, but loud enough to be heard.*) Not if we use crêpe paper.

SUE.

Some entertainment will be needed, too, for about fifteen minutes between the dinner and the meeting.

EDITH.

Well, I'll go along with just about anything except a solo by Selma Shacklemeyer. She can't carry a tune in a suitcase! And why she's always asked to sing solos, I'll never know!

THE COMMITTEE MEETING 11

DORIS.

There's always Jimmy Gentry and his saxophone.

EDITH.

He's even more off-key than Selma Shacklemeyer!

SUE.

I think it's nice if we use the talent we have right in our own church.

DORIS.

What about the quartet?

EDITH.

Good grief! It's bad enough when they sing at the worship service on Sunday morning. Let's not force them onto the congregational meeting, too.

DORIS.

I think they're rather good. My brother sings tenor, you know.

AMY.

Oh, I think they're very good. They *harmonize* so well. I always say when you want to hear some very good *harmonizing*, just call on our quartet.

MARY.

Yes, yes! I'll have to go along with you there, Amy.

SUE.

I don't think Selma sings so badly.

DORIS.

And what's wrong with Jimmy Gentry's saxophone? He does very well for a ten-year-old.

AMY.

I think the quartet should definitely be asked.

MARY.

Oh, so do I!

THE COMMITTEE MEETING

EDITH.

If Selma Shacklemeyer sings, I'm not coming!

(*Everyone breaks into loud chattering and arguing again until* SUE *realizes her position as chairman and blows her whistle. Everyone jumps and faces her.*)

SUE.

Girls! Shall we move on now? Publicity is the next item.

EDITH.

Posters are always good, that is, if you can find anyone around here who can make some decent-looking ones.

DORIS.

Telephone committees are always good.

AMY.

And announcements in all the Sunday School classes. Announcements are so *informative*. I always say if you want to *inform* anybody about anything, just make an announcement.

MARY.

You're absolutely right, Amy, absolutely right!

EDITH.

I say we should have some posters!

DORIS.

Telephone committees are very thorough and reach more people. A lot of people won't bother to look at a poster, but everyone will answer the phone.

AMY.

I always say nothing beats a good announcement.

SUE.

Well, that's all of the committees, girls. The men will be in charge of the business meeting.

Edith.

Now there's a mistake if I ever heard one! Men in charge of the meeting! No wonder they last all night! Men don't know the first thing about conducting a meeting.

Doris.

They're always getting off the subject.

Amy.

They should take some pointers from our meetings.

Doris.

Definitely! We always manage to conduct our meetings in an orderly manner. But men have no sense of order at all. Like the time George Thompson was discussing a place for the men's retreat. He got to talking about Lake Larson where his father always goes fishing. He talked for ten minutes about fishing at Lake Larson!

Mary.

Oh, my husband always goes fishing at Lake Larson. He says it's the best place around here for good bass.

Edith.

Not according to my Harry. He goes bass fishing on the river.

Amy.

Oh, but Lake Larson is such a *lovely* place with such nice trees and picnic tables. My garden club goes there every year for its annual picnic. I always say if you want a *lovely* picnic spot, just drive up to Lake Larson.

(*Everyone bursts into noisy chattering again for a moment until* Sue *is forced to blow her whistle again.*)

Sue.

Girls! Now that we've had our discussion, we'll appoint our committee chairmen, and then we'll be ready to go to work. Now, who would like to take charge of the Food Committee?

(*Everyone glances slyly at everyone else.*)

AMY.

(*Suddenly.*) Why don't you do that, Edith? You're such a good *organizer!* I always say if you need a good *organizer,* just call on Edith.

MARY.

Oh, yes! I've always said that, too, Amy.

EDITH.

Absolutely not! It's utterly impossible! Oh, I assure you I'd like to do something, but I have painters and paperhangers coming this week, and my sister is getting married next month, and my family will just throw everything in my lap. But I was thinking of Eleanor. She's good at this sort of thing, and she likes *my* macaroni and cheese!

MARY.

Yes, yes! Eleanor! Doesn't she usually bring devilled eggs?

DORIS.

She makes fairly good coffee, too. Not as good as mine, of course, but certainly drinkable.

EDITH.

(*Writing in notes.*) Eleanor, Chairman of the Food Committee.

SUE.

Now for decorations.

(*Everyone looks slyly at everyone else.*)

AMY.

(*Suddenly.*) How about you, Doris? You're so *artistic* with colored crêpe paper. I always say if you want something done *artistically* with colored crêpe paper, just call on Doris.

MARY.

Oh, yes! You do such *odd* things with crêpe paper, Doris!

DORIS.

Well, I'm sure I'd be happy to, except that lately I've had such a time with my cough. (*Coughs.*) Ever since that horrible attack of flu I had last week (*cough*) I just haven't completely recovered. My doctor told me not to use my voice very much (*cough*) or over-exert myself. (*Cough.*) He said if I wasn't careful (*cough*) I'd run myself down and have to stay in bed for a week. (*Cough.*) I'm sure you girls can understand.

SUE.

Oh, of course, Doris. Perhaps you shouldn't have come out in this chilly night air.

DORIS.

Oh, I couldn't let you down, Sue! I do want to do my part. (*Cough.*) But right now I'm afraid it's simply out of the question. (*Cough.*) I was thinking about Clara. Doesn't she make all the decorations for the hospital parties? (*Cough.*)

MARY.

Oh, yes! Clara! The patients just love her decorations. She should definitely be in charge of our decorations.

SUE.

But isn't she always terribly busy?

EDITH.

I'm sure she'll be more than glad to help. (*Writing in notes.*) Clara, Decorations Committee Chairman!

SUE.

Now we need someone to line up the entertainment.

(*Silence.*)

AMY.

(Suddenly.) I think that's an excellent job for you, Sue! You know so many *entertaining* people, being in the choir and all. I always say that you know more *entertaining* people than anyone else I know!

MARY.

Yes! Yes! That's definitely the job for you, Sue!

SUE.

Well, I appreciate your confidence in me, girls, but you see, my sister and her five children are coming to visit us this weekend, and I have so much to do to get ready for them. Why, I won't even be able to go to choir practice! And then, when they do come, they take up every spare moment I have. I hope you understand, girls. I'd really like to help, but . . . I know! I know who would be just perfect for this. Ann!

AMY.

Ann! Of course! A very good choice!

EDITH.

(Writing in notes.) Chairman of Entertainment Committee, Ann! And she'd better not come up with Selma Shacklemeyer!

SUE.

And now publicity.

(Silence.)

AMY.

I know who would be just ideal for publicity! You, Mary!

MARY.

Oh, yes, I . . . *(Suddenly realizes that she is the one* AMY *has named.)* Oh, no! Amy! I couldn't! Really, I couldn't! I'm going away for the weekend to visit my Aunt Elsie in Cleveland. We've been promising her we'd come for a visit for so long, and the weather forecast says this weekend is going to be perfect. I just can't disappoint my Aunt Elsie!

AMY.

Of course not, Mary. I understand.

MARY.

What about Evelyn?

AMY.

Evelyn! Of course! Evelyn is so *professional.* I've always said that Evelyn is one of the most *professional* people I know.

EDITH.

(*Writing.*) Evelyn, Chairman of Publicity.

SUE.

Well, that takes care of everything, girls. I'll call all these chairmen tomorrow and tell them to get to work right away. We certainly finished our business in a short time!

DORIS.

Of course! We know how to conduct an efficient meeting. And just look at what we've accomplished! All the committee chairmen have been chosen.

AMY.

Now we can all go to the dinner-meeting and enjoy ourselves, knowing that everything is in good hands.

MARY.

Doesn't it make you feel good to know that you're really doing something worthwhile? I'm always so glad to be called on.

DORIS.

As I said, girls, it's the women who get things done, who pave the way, who hear the call and obey!

SUE.

Yes, and I'm sure if any of these chairmen need help we'll all be ready to volunteer.

Edith.

Well, I've got to get home and start looking at that paint color chart.

Doris.

(*Remembering to cough.*) I think I'll go right home and go to bed. I don't think I'll ever get over this flu.

Amy.

It's been such a *lovely* meeting, Sue. I've always said that you hold such *lovely* meetings. If you need my help with anything, just call on me.

Mary.

Good night, Sue. I've got to rush home and start packing. We want to get an early start for Cleveland in the morning.

Sue.

(*As everyone gets up and starts to leave.*) Good night, girls. I'm glad you all could come, and you've all been so helpful! Good night!

(*Everyone leaves, saying good night,* Doris *coughing, etc.*)

THE END

MUSIC USE NOTE

Licensees are solely responsible for obtaining formal written permission from copyright owners to use copyrighted music in the performance of this play and are strongly cautioned to do so. If no such permission is obtained by the licensee, then the licensee must use only original music that the licensee owns and controls. Licensees are solely responsible and liable for all music clearances and shall indemnify the copyright owners of the play(s) and their licensing agent, Samuel French, against any costs, expenses, losses and liabilities arising from the use of music by licensees. Please contact the appropriate music licensing authority in your territory for the rights to any incidental music.

IMPORTANT BILLING AND CREDIT REQUIREMENTS

If you have obtained performance rights to this title, please refer to your licensing agreement for important billing and credit requirements.

www.ingramcontent.com/pod-product-compliance
Lightning Source LLC
Chambersburg PA
CBHW050124020526
44112CB00035B/2467